Team Member

I0485498

Learn To Be A Great Team Member And Be An Important Part Of Your Workgroup

By

Meenakshi Narang

I

Meenakshi Narang

Table of Contents

INTRODUCTION..4

Chapter 1: The Team....................................5

Being a Team Member.......................................6

Comprehending Team Objectives.................8

Chapter 2: Understanding Team Roles With
Belbin Theory 9

Active Roles 10

Performing Roles 11

Thinking Roles...12

What Kind of Team Member are You?........14

Chapter 3: How To Be A Great Team Player.27

Assertiveness: A Significant team playing
technique..31

What is Assertiveness 31

Assertiveness for Team Playing...............32

Behavior of an Assertive Team Member
....33

Chapter 4: Be An Assertive Team Player 34

The Origin of Assertiveness........................36

Grow and Preen these Habits........................38

Chapter 5: Be An Inherent Solution Finder 41

Step 1 – Know The Root Cause 42

Step 2 – Surf the Facts 43

Step 3 - Sort the Problem 44

Step 4 – Develop Ideas 44

Step 5 –Choose the Idea and weigh up...45

Step 6 – Inherent Planning 45

Step 7 –Popularize Your Idea....................45

Step 8 – Execution 46

Chapter 6: How To Be The Powerful Link Of Your Workgroup...47

What May Hamper Your Growth in Your Team 50

INTRODUCTION

It isn't easy to be a part of a team. It takes effort and skills to be a great team member and contribute to the workgroup. This eBook, titled "Learn to Be a Great Team Member and Be an Important Part of your Workgroup" will help in polishing soft skills to be one of the powerful members of the team.

This eBook includes effective ways of understanding team's objectives and become a star team member.

Happy Reading!

Chapter 1: The Team

The literal meaning of team is "group or groups of people who share a common objective, remain committed to solving the problems, take correct decisions and empower the goals".

The team is a 'cohesive group' that works in unison in the same environment. It is led by a group of people who instead of working towards their individual goal, work for a collective purpose.

Team playing benefits organization as well as the team members. Having a team helps an organization by -

- Improving its productivity

- Enhancing the creativity and bringing innovation

- Better employees' motivation and commitment

- Better usage of resources

- High levels of involvement

- Cohesive working atmosphere

Being a Team Member

Team playing is part of most of our commercial or non-commercial activities. In the present scenario, team playing is at its best.

If you are also part of a team at your workplace, it goes without saying – you have to be the best in order to carve a distinct niche in your team. Being a team member means -

- You have a shared network of communication

- You have to accept accountability without any qualms

- You have to work with co-operation

- You have to anticipate on personal and professional level

- You have to support other team members

- You have to learn self-development

- You have to develop a common 'team-goal' and understand it well

- You have to remain involved with team's decision-making

- You have to be patient supportive

Comprehending Team Objectives

Unified teams do not get ready in a single day. Good teams are the resultant of team manager's hard work and foresight.

Every team has a goal to follow. As a team member, understand team's goals and work in tandem. As a team member, follow the team's mission and maintain its cohesiveness.

Chapter 2: Understanding Team Roles With Belbin Theory

A good team has well defined roles for its members. When all team members execute their responsibilities collectively, the team emerges to be a winner.

However, things may not be as simple as they seem to be. How often you have felt that while you are trying your best to fulfill your responsibilities, other team members are evasive and not delivering optimally? The experts are of an opinion that different team members tend to have the subjective approach towards team roles. Dr. Meredith Belbin defined nine team roles for team's success.

To be a good and a balanced team member, understand the Belbin model. Keeping in mind other relevant factors, this information can be used as a guide–

The nine team roles identified by Belbin are divided into three groups –

1.   Active Roles

2.   Performing Roles

3.   Thinking Roles

These nine team-roles are -

Active Roles
1.   **Shapers** – These team members are challengers who lead the improvisation. They are dynamically extrovert and question the conventions. They explore

all possibilities and find the best possible solutions. Their drawback is their argumentative nature.

2. **Implementers** – They get things rolling by transforming ideas into actions. They work systematically but are conservative in their mind set. These team members tend to be rigid and resistant in their approach.

3. **Finishers** – These people complete projects to perfection and leave no room for mistakes. They are particular about the deadlines and are conscientious in their approach. They may fuss unnecessarily to meet the perfection.

Performing Roles
1. **Coordinators** – They are leaders of the team who guide other team members towards the objective. They listen carefully and can identify each member's worth.

2.   **Team Workers** – Team workers are the support of the team and fulfill the work of diplomatic negotiators. They work towards keeping the team united and remain popular with masses. However, they can be indecisive and maintain non-committed approach.

3.   **Investigators** – Invigilators always remain curious and innovative. They are extroverts and good negotiators. They carry an optimistic persona but tend to lose their enthusiasm soon.

Thinking Roles

1.   **Planters** – These members are the idea generators. They are brilliant indeed, but they prefer working within their cocoon. On a downside, they are low on communication and often nurture impractical ideas.

2.   **Evaluators** – They are good at analyzing with astuteness. They shrewdly weigh all the ups and the downs of the situation.

3. **Specialists** – These members are knowledgeable and carry wonderful skill set. They remain committed to their area of expertise.

Knowing about these team roles will help in knowing team's constitution and other team members' behavior. Team skills can be built after understanding these roles.

Answer the following questions for better understanding of team's goal –

*   Why the team has been formulated?

*   What is the goal of this project?

*   What deadline needs to be met?

*   Who will be implementing / executing ideas?

*   What roles do I have to play in the team?

What Kind of Team Member are You?

This is Parker Team Player Survey that would help in identifying the kind of team player you are. This would help you in honing your skills and enhance your team playing skills.

Instructions:

Understand that this is a survey, and there could be dual answers. Answer these questions to know the kind of team member you are.

There are 18 incomplete sentences with four choices of selecting answers. Rank the endings in the preference order. Number 4 should be placed for the most applicable ending, going downward towards number 1 for the least applicable choice. Do not use 1,2,3,4 numbers more than once for avoiding a tie-like situation.

Here goes the survey –

1. At the time of team meetings, I prefer -

a)   Providing technical information or data to the team

b)   Keeping focus on team's goal and mission

c)   Ensuring everyone's participation in discussion

d)   Raising queries

2. As a team leader, I prefer -

a)   Making achievable targets

b)   Building positive team atmosphere

c)   Making my disagreement vocal

d)   Rendering advice according to my expertise

3.   When stressed out, I prefer -

a)   Using humor for reducing tension

b)   Directly communicate with my team over how I feel

c)   Losing temper and vent out my feelings

d)   Sharing problems with outsiders

4.   At the time of conflicts within team, I prefer -

a)   Having an honest and a straight discussion

b)   Reasoning who is right and who is wrong

c)   Changing the fundamental structure of the team for resolving the conflicts

d)   Breaking the tension with humor or sarcasm

5. My team mates consider me –

a) Fact oriented

b) Pliable

c) Encouraging

d) Blunt

6. Sometimes I behave –

a) Extremely stubborn

b) Lazy and laid-back

c) Pompous

d) Restricted in perception

7. When situation is not very rosy within the team, I –

a) Lend a patient ear to the problem and participate wholeheartedly

b) Discuss openly on the problems

c) Strive to work harder and get more information

d) Revisit the mission of the project

8. For me, it is very risky to –

a) Question team's working habits

b) Encourage team to scale greater standard of working

c) Leave my comfort zone

d) Give feedback to other teammates

9. My teammates sometimes consider me to be –

a) An uncompromising worker

b) A failure in assessing team's goals

c) Casual about accomplishing the job seriously

d) Moaner

10. According to me, for solving team problems, it is mandatory to –

a)   Cooperate with all teammates

b)   Possess excellent listening skills

c)   Pose tough questions

d)   Have impressive data

11. At the time of forming a new team =

a)   I go out of way to meet and know all team members

b)   I question sharply about team's work-method and goals

c)   I try to know what is expected of me

d)   I seek precision over team's fundamental mission

12. I often make my teammates feel –

a) Untruthful

b) Guilty for not matching my work standards

c) Opinionated and short-sighted

d) Callous in professional approach

13. I consider a team leader to be –

a) An efficient solution provider

b) An establisher of long term goals and short term objectives

c) A decision-maker r

d) A Challenger of conventional ideas

14. The decisions in team should rely on –

a) Team's goals and mission

b) Team members

c) An open estimation of the issues

d)   Individual performance

15.   At times, I -

a)   Consider team as an autonomous assemblage

b)   Act in favor of team's devil

c)   Fail to witness team's effective process

d)   Exaggerate strategic tasks and their accomplishments

16.   I am known to my team mates as -

a)   An independent team player

b)   A dependable person

c)   A creative and an imaginative worker

d)   A participative team member

17.   Usually I am –

a) Hardworking and responsible

b) Committed and pliable

c) Humorous and full of enthusiasm

d) Honest and reliable

18. I get annoyed with my team mates when they don't –

a) Keep a track on team's goals and objectives

b) Gel with one another while working

c) Raise objections to faulty process and disagreeable decisions

d) Accomplish their tasks on time

Results

Transfer answers of this questionnaire to the below-mentioned table and get ready for the assessment. Take care of the order of letters for each question. Enter the numbers carefully. The total of all four columns would come out to be 180.

Question   Contributor   Collaborator Communicator   Challenger

1. a. __   b. __   c. __   d. __

2. d. __   a. __   b. __   c. __

3. c. __   d. __   a. __   b. __

4. b. __   c. __   d. __   a. __

5. a. __   b. __   c. __   d. __

6. d. __   a. __   b. __   c. __

7. c. __   d. __   a. __   b. __

8. b. __   c. __   d. __   a. __

9. a. __   b. __   c. __   d. __

10. d. __   a. __   b. __   c. __

11. c. __   d. __   a. __   b. __

12. b. __   c. __   d. __   a. __

13. a. __   b. __   c. __   d. __

14. d. ___   a. ___   b. ___   c. ___

15. b. ___   d. ___   a. ___   b. ___

16. c. ___   c. ___   d. ___   a. ___

17. a. ___   b. ___   c. ___   d. ___

18. d. ___   a. ___   b. ___   c. ___

Totals ___   ___   ___   ___ = 180

Are You a Good Team Player?

Professional teams are made for varied purposes. There could be a one-time project or an ongoing one. Team playing helps in accomplishing greater tasks in lesser time with the help of group's combined effort and energy.

Being part of a team can be wondrous for your career. You may have proven your caliber as an individual worker, however, your ability to work cohesively in a team will need accreditation to take you to next level. If you can gel well within a team, you will certainly leave an impressive professional impact.

An earnest effort to be part of a team, would build your character, make you empathetic, and take you closer to your aspiration.

In nutshell, being a good team member is important because –

- Your group effort is going to be more impressive and effective than your individual effort.
- You would prove your merit to not just yourself but others too.
- You learn to tackle your responsibilities; and are liable to many others. You cannot just wash your hands off by taking individual decisions.
- You learn to find collective solutions to maintain team's sanctity.

- You learn to act not with an air of superiority but with an empathetic approach.
- You learn to push your work standards further, consequently helping the rest of the team members to work even better.
- You learn that you and your team's success are equally important for one another.

Chapter 3: How To Be A Great Team Player

Yes, we sincerely want you to be a great team player. Read ahead the 10 listed qualities for becoming a prized member of a team.

1. Reliability

Be reliable so that your team manager can count on you. Be consistent in showing your reliability. Be an unswerving performer instead of being an abrupt or unpredictable one.

2. Communication

Poor communication leads to poor expression. This would result in failed conveyance of ideas and thoughts. Speak expressively and transmit the ideas clearly. Be confident, and positive in your communication.

3. Listening

You ought to develop enough patience to be a good listener. Those who cannot be listeners often lose a valid point.

4. Participation

Be an active and agile participant to be part of meetings and discussions. Your muted or lethargic behavior may act against you. Your initiative is going to endorse your effort.

5. Sharing

You cannot afford to keep everything to yourself. You ought to share and disseminate all that you gather. This will maintain the objective of team building and make you earn others' trust. You can foster informal sharing for keeping all in the loop of information.

6. Cooperation

Cooperating is not about following someone blindly. It is about working in tandem with others. To be a good team player, learn to be cooperative. There might be differences at times, but the trick lies in finding a middle way to resolves the issue.

7. Flexibility

Don't be rigid lest you would close every possible door of negotiation. Being in a team would mean encountering dynamic circumstances that would demand you to be pliable with opinions and decisions.

8. Commitment

Commitment should be your middle name. Do what you say and allow your commitment to be your USP. Your commitment will be infectious, and your associates will take your word seriously. This trait will help you shine brighter and scale greater heights.

9. Result oriented

You are in team for solving a problem. Be result oriented and do not dilly-dally the process. Do not dwell on the problem too long in a hope to solve it in a better way. Unnecessary sitting over the problem will make it enormous.

10.   Respectful

Team playing has no room for rudeness.
Your personal dealing with your team
members will establish your rapport and
impression. Treat others with respect and
honor their opinion even if you don't
agree. Understand people and their
situations. Take help of humor and
healthy sarcasm to tackle a dicey
situation.

Your winning as a team member will not
come by defeating your opponent. It
would come by being a motivator.

Assertiveness: A Significant team playing technique

What is Assertiveness

There are several self-development
courses and training programs designed
to encourage assertiveness. However,
defining assertiveness continues to be a
challenge. Usually, its definition is
restricted to the alternative behavior

patterns like aggression and submission that arise due to the absence of assertiveness. However, studies show that the key to any positive and productive relationship is assertiveness.

In the absence of assertive skills, there is a good chance that people resort to aggressive or passive communication that results in a strained relationship. It can affect trust and intimacy between two individuals to a greater extent.

Assertiveness for Team Playing
When you understand the effects of the absence of assertiveness, defining it becomes easier. In simple words, assertiveness can be defined as an honest and a direct communication that aims at respecting the needs, rights and emotions of the other person.

There are several attempts to define the term assertiveness in the dictionary. Most of them are misleading as they indicate "confidence", "dogmatism" and "positivity". In reality, assertiveness is a lot more than that.

Many times, assertiveness is also mistaken as being dominating and resistant. Assertiveness is not about being overpowering, angry, emotional or even about forcing your opinions. It is the ability to be free from fear, to be honest and to trust.

Behavior of an Assertive Team Member
An individual is assertive when he:

- Can be direct or honest
- Can negotiate
- Can balance the concept of give and take
- Can have his needs fulfilled without disrespecting others' needs
- Can set boundaries and say "no" when necessary
- Can identify his or her mistakes

Chapter 4: Be An Assertive Team Player

The secret to success in many facets of our lives is assertiveness. Assertiveness plays a very important role in our workplace where we are expected to use our skills of communicating, leading and negotiating. When it comes to the personal space in our lives, assertiveness helps us solve problems and resolve several conflicts. With these benefits, on an individual level, assertiveness is one of the factors that make us feel good in general.

When an individual is assertive -stress and fear gets eliminated. These two factors are constantly a part of personal and professional lives in the form of demanding seniors, dissatisfied customers and also uncooperative co-workers. The result of these relationships (based on fear and stress) is fight and negative reactions. The defense mechanism in case of such relationships ranges from avoiding, fighting, and bullying to manipulating people.

If individuals can be assertive, a lot of uneasiness, mental complexities and exhaustion can be avoided. Acquiring assertive skills will help you stay in a relationship without any fear, irrespective of what the other individual is looking for. It is possible to control emotions and hold them back instead of reacting negatively. It also lets you see other people in the same light that you see yourself in.

Although assertiveness is not an ultimate remedy for resolving issues; it is a primary social skill that helps promote positive human behavior.

The Origin of Assertiveness

Assertiveness is a skill that most people are born with. If you start with the stage of infancy, you can observe that the way babies relate to the world is completely loving, open and honest. However, when people are not as open and loving in return, it triggers fear. The concept of danger that never existed before begins to grow. In order to protect yourself from these dangers, you are tutored by your parents. These protective skills are usually imparted out of experience. So, in a way, we are trained throughout our lives to be non-assertive in many ways.

Assertiveness is a skill that comes with conscious effort and practice. Assertiveness is undoubtedly a skill that can help us deal with several situations, in and out of work. Those who lack confidence can overcome stress by being assertive. Assertiveness aims at helping people unlearn various behaviors from their past and then reprogram themselves. Techniques like modifying self-talk, the ABC technique, visualization, scripting and trigger setting are employed to improve assertiveness.

After developing skills of assertiveness, you as a team member will be

- Self-expecting

- Self-confident

- Intellectually empowered

- Attractive

- Independent

- Active and Assertive

- A switch from dependence to independence

- Able to handle criticism

Grow and Preen these Habits

For being an integral part of the team, don't outgrow these habits. These habits will contribute to the success of a mission, and consequently in the enhancement of your glory. We call these traits as habits so that they are formed for long term benefitting.

Considering others before self – This sounds simple but would require a herculean task. Don't work for your personal mission but for the collective cause. It could be as simple as offering menial help to your associate in documentation. Overcome the fear of not offering help lest someone might say yes to your help.

Reflecting your actions – You might be thinking that too much of reflecting might make you over-analyze things. But developing this habit will harness your talent optimally. Pondering over what you have done and what you ought to do will minimize the chances of probable mistakes and ensure the success of the team. This becomes even more important as, however, big or small a team may be, the onus of its success lies on all members equally.

Staying Prepared – This habit is going to benefit immense. If you remain inherently organized, you will never regret. Being planned and prepared will effortlessly take you closer to team's objective.

Being curious – Considering you to be super knowledgeable is always fatal. Don't think like that. Rather, assume that you have yet to learn. Don't take your training for granted and remain curious to unravel knowledge. Your quest to know more will thrust you towards progression.

Try and Try Again – Comfort is always restrictive. The moment you decide to remain within your comfort zone, you cease growth. Strive harder and step out of your comfort zone to exploit your optimum potential.

Chapter 5: Be An Inherent Solution Finder

The team needs problem-solving members. If you are good at finding solutions, you can rule the roost. Take your problems as milestones to make you succeed further.

Sometimes in the grit of packed schedules you may have tried to solve the problem in a jiffy, and realize later that there could have been a better solution.

Be a logical thinker and identify the root-cause of the problem in a systematic way. Here we tell you the secret of being a problem solver with the help of 'Simplex Process'. This includes strategies and tools that would make problem-solving an easier task.

Step 1 – Know The Root Cause

While some problems make an obvious appearance, others remain hidden and need to be identified. Identification of the problem is an important aspect that would help in problem-solving. Tackling the problem close to their inception would help in preventing emergencies.

The below-listed techniques are beneficial in multiple ways –

- PEST Analysis – It helps in identifying the dynamics of 'what' and 'how'; and how it would affect the team.

- Risk Analysis – It helps in identifying impending risks that may affect the business goal.
- Failure Modes and Effects Analysis – It helps in identifying probable points of failure that would lead towards the bigger problem.

After Action Reviews – It helps in taking a futuristic approach.

Step 2 – Surf the Facts

After identifying the problem, you need to have adequate information to tackle it further. You need to ponder –

- Who are involved in the problem?

- What efforts have been taken to resolve this problem earlier?

- What do others think about the problem?

There is no need to resolve the problem hastily else its solution would fail on the scale of consistency. Research the problem methodically.

Step 3 - Sort the Problem

The classification of the problem will become easier for you, as you have now enough information about it. Classifying the problem also includes defining it precisely for knowing its scope. The technique of 'Cause and Effect Analysis' will be of great use in segregating problem's symptoms from its elementary causes.

Step 4 – Develop Ideas

Now it is time to generate ideas for seeking the solution of the problem in a flexible way. Consider multiple aspects for an apt solution. One best way to generate idea is via traditional / reversal brainstorming where a range of creative ideas are juggled to find the best possible way out.

Step 5 –Choose the Idea and weigh up

Brainstorm well and gather a range of relevant ideas. There would be ample options to select from that would lead to serious evaluation. Don't act hastily and start discarding ideas blindly.
Contemplate all the options and finalize the best idea.

Step 6 – Inherent Planning

Mere evaluation of idea will not solve the problem. This would be followed by implementation. However, meticulous planning is needed for this.

Step 7 –Popularize Your Idea

Since you are part of a team, here onwards starts an important task of vending your idea to other team members. Contemplate all the options beforehand to counter the resistance. Conduct enough research to make your idea foolproof. Be pliable enough to alter your idea.

Step 8 – Execution

Now is the stage of implementation. This is the final stage of the problem-solving strategy that would seem worthwhile, especially after all the brainstorming.

Chapter 6: How To Be The Powerful Link Of Your Workgroup

Good teams are made of collective aspirations and motivation. This goes on to achieve colossal tasks. What may remain unaccomplished can be achieved by being part of a unified group. Become indispensable link in the chain of your work team by following below listed ways –

Set an exemplary standard- Don't think microscopically about your productivity and performance. Rather, work hard ceaselessly to convey your passion and commitment. Be your best and deliver your 100 percent. Set an exemplary standard by being a perfectionist...success will ultimately follow you.

Hone your strengths – Hone your strengths and capabilities. If you do not allow your talent to come to the fore, you will not be doing justice to your commitments. Improve and innovate yourself to take your team to the higher levels. What may seem a selfish act, on a larger level, is a way to serve your team.

Emit positivity – You can shine and dazzle brighter by being positive and a practical team member. Everyone likes to bond with a positive person for infectious optimism. Instead of being a negative and a complainer, be upbeat.

Interact frequently – Don't be an introvert team member. There may be a volcano of talent simmering inside you, but you ought to interact with others. Your positive interactions will make you productive. Interact by praising, encouraging, appreciating, recognizing and energizing.

Revere the team spirit – Your individual performance deserves to be harnessed for development of the team and team spirit. Keep your personal interest ego aside for team's objective.

Bond well – Teaming is all about grouping. And this must be supported by bonding positively with all team members. Having a healthy relationship with other teammates will certainly make you a scintillating star. Despite being a smart worker, the importance of bonding with others cannot be negated.

Establish trust – Trust can bring great bonhomie in the team and strengthen the interpersonal skills. When you will be trusted, you will be heard and even believed. Be integral, consistent, transparent, honest, and dependable as a team member.

Be humble – Humility is a winning tool. Your humility will take you places by learning and improving your skills. Being humble will prevent conflict, if any, and constructive discussion will be encouraging. Realize the power of humility and tap its potential.

What May Hamper Your Growth in Your Team

Yeah…you have learned enough to be an outstanding team member. Now, take note of all those mistakes you are likely to make. Each of the listed mistakes can push you back to square one. So be cautious.

1. Taking planning as an event instead of a process

Planning cannot happen in a switch-on-switch-off mode. It isn't an instance but a process that goes on until the desired results are experienced. Considering planning to be an event will take off its objective and will fizzle out soon. Planning should be routine to maintain the consistency.

2. Ignoring timing factor

While everything is being perfectly attended by you, ill timing may mar your effort. Keep a tab on some sensitive processes like budgeting, and appraisals to have a timely planning or execution. Your sense of timing will certainly be appreciated by your team leader.

3. Disregarding relevant research

You may be missing that extra edge by not researching. While rest of the team may be harping on the information provided by the leader, leap ahead and go an extra mile to research on own. The intent should be to appear smarter and more informed by having better knowledge.

4.   I'll do it alone

Don't forget you are a team member. Of course, you are liable to your personal aspirations don't forget your team. Don't commit the grave mistake of burdening your lone shoulders with responsibilities. This may crumble down your spirit. Instead, work in tandem with the rest of the team members Do what you are best at, and share tasks with other team members.

5.   Foggy communication

Please...don't sulk or brood while in a team. This would soon alienate you from your team mates and damage your repute. Healthy communication will build not just your individual standing but also professional spirit. Foster healthy communication at all levels.

6. Hiding your cards

It is natural for you to feel secretive about the idea you have been nurturing. But this can be harmful. Since nothing is personal in a team, this kind of secretiveness may backfire. Rather, reveal your plan or idea clearly so that you can work over it without worry. Moreover, the early revelation of the idea will sort of patent your idea.

7. Sitting on the plan for long

You might consider sitting too long over some plan to give it a best shot. This strategy won't work in a team. Delayed working can cost you the project, and someone rapid may take away all the accolades.

8. Battling change

Believe in 'change is constant'. As a team member, you may have to alter or overhaul your plan. Don't resist this. Be open-minded and take the change in your stride.

9.   Setting impracticable milestones

Don't get swayed by aspirations and set impractical milestone. Know your compatibility quotient, take a clear understanding of the magnitude of the project and then state your commitment.

10.   Deficiency of personal accountability

Be gracious enough to take accountability of your mistakes. Don't play the blame game to shift your wrong doings. Mistakes are normal and must not weigh down your enterprise. By taking personal accountability, you would be proving your caliber.

www.ingramcontent.com/pod-product-compliance
Lightning Source LLC
Chambersburg PA
CBHW071001180526
45168CB00003B/1245